THE LUNCHEON
OF THE BOATING PARTY

Stewart Conn was born in Glasgow in 1936, and brought up in Ayrshire. Married with two sons, he now lives in Edinburgh. His previous volumes of poems *Stoats in the Sunlight* and *Under the Ice* received Scottish Arts Council Awards, while *An Ear to the Ground* was a Poetry Book Society Choice. His latest two poetry books are both published by Bloodaxe, *In the Kibble Palace: New & Selected Poems* (1987) and *The Luncheon of the Boating Party* (1992).

His most recent stage plays have been *Hugh Miller*, winner of a 1988 Edinburgh Festival Fringe Award, *By the Pool*, given its American première by Cleveland Play House, Ohio, last spring, and *The Dominion of Fancy*, commissioned for Pitlochry Festival Theatre's 1992 season.

STEWART CONN

The Luncheon of
the Boating Party

BLOODAXE BOOKS

ISBN: 1 85224 142 X

First published 1992 by
Bloodaxe Books Ltd,
P.O. Box 1SN,
Newcastle upon Tyne NE99 1SN.

Bloodaxe Books Ltd acknowledges
the financial assistance of Northern Arts.

Cover printing by Index Print, Newcastle upon Tyne.

Cover reproduction by V & H Reprographics, Newcastle upon Tyne.

Printed in Great Britain by
Bell & Bain Limited, Glasgow, Scotland.

for Judy

Acknowledgements

The title sequence, with 'Renoir in Orkney', was first published as a 'Weekender' feature in the *Glasgow Herald*. 'Starling' and 'Bittern' are two of *Three Bird Songs* set to music by David Dorward.

Thanks are also due to the editors of *Aquarius, The Best of Scottish Poetry* (Chambers, 1989), *Cencrastus, Chapman, The Edinburgh Review, Gairfish, The Living Poet* (BBC Radio 3), *London Magazine, New Writing Scotland, The Observer, The Scotsman, Six poètes écossais* (Éditions Telo Martius, 1991), *Spectrum, The Sunday Times* and *Verse* where poems in this book previously appeared, though not always in their present form.

Contents

II.

I.

Wild Flowers

I didn't know *lupinus polyphyllus* as such, in those days:
simply that our manse garden was rampant with displays
of varying blue; nor that this converging in colour
of massed spikes, year after year, was a reverting to nature.

Oblivious, we lay in their ribbed and scented dens,
bees blundering by, under clouds of chiffon. As intense
were the stained-glass windows we gazed at on Sundays,
the congregation dwindling – successive generations

heading for housing schemes, but still the appeals
for the fabric fund, the carillon of bells;
the burden ever greater, for fewer to bear.
Compare *epilobium angustifolium*, similarly

tall-stemmed, but a looser, fluffier flower,
its purple spires pointed out by my mother
when we went for runs in the family car, till we'd cry,
'Guess what, rosebay willow-herb!' Found primarily

on disused railways, it proliferates where factories were;
reminder of jobs lost, of bitterness and despair.
In abundance, willow-herb and lupin demonstrate
the slow dereliction of Church and State.

Burial Mound

Entering Maeshowe we have to bend double
for the narrow passage which brings us
to the main chamber, in whose recesses
lodged the bones and ashes
of the dead. Torch flitting from ceiling to wall

my guide recites the history of the place,
revealing chiselled runes
on slate slabs, before the beam moves on.
Hesitantly I ask, could she please
cast light again on the inscriptions:

Ingibiorg is the fairest of women;
Hervuntnr of the hard axe carved these –
I ought not to have spoken.
She stops abruptly and with a frozen
clearing of the throat, recommences

from the beginning, without expression
but faster, permitting no further
interruption. Later she lets me examine
briefly the rows of stick-figures,
leads me to daylight again.

Tonight we lie, you and I, darkness a dome
overhead. At least we are together,
our love a live thing, this room
not yet ransacked by whatever invader
will carve here, as on cold stone, his name.

Boat Trip

The motor-boat cuts a swathe across the Sound
as on taut silk, to deposit us on the Island.
We head for a vantage point, tiptoeing between
gulls' nests, each with its speckled contents,
ignored by the parent birds – whereas terns or skuas
would instantly have had the scalps off us.

We munch cress sandwiches, the melons we brought.
Pairs of eider go burbling past. Seals
flip-flop from the rock, keeping cool.
Morar emerges from haze. On our return journey
we pass through tangles of *lasagna verdi*
and whorls of liquorice, still unharvested.

Later, in an oblong of heat trapped
by the cottage wall, you could close your eyes
and be in Provence almost: the bouquet
of bramble wine, aroma of wild thyme,
scarcely comprehensible in conjunction
with the peat stacks, those peaks on the skyline.

Make the most of it. Soon it will become
another memory, a fiction of its own.
That night the storm breaks; and I hear
Flaubert howl, knowing his Emma, no more
than artifice, an array of imagined syllables,
would long after his death remain alive and real.

Whiteness

The cherry tree at our window sways in time
to the concerto we're listening to, or so it seems
at heightened intervals – the bars between,
harmonious variations on a theme
buoyant enough to allow for improvisation.

Look, there they go again: the branches bounce
with the *arpeggio*, then coyly flounce
as the woodwind reiterate love's innocence,
all building joyously to the last reprise,
music and blossom trembling in one breeze;

until oddly, this serves as a reminder
that in cultures other than ours,
colour values may vary. I shiver
involuntarily, recalling the Toho
Company's *Macbeth* of four Festivals ago,

in which complicitous branches swayed (or so
it seemed) as like a deadly lattice,
round Banquo's neck we saw the bright blades cross;
while later, still the pure white petals fell,
as the headless king descended into hell.

White Cleuch

Above White Cleuch, two arctic hares
lie on open ground. Legs stiffly crossed,
pure white from nose to scut,
they are like relics, hallucinatory almost.

But something is wrong. They are too still.
Alongside each creature, as we draw near,
we detect a ripple of intestines
packed with strychnine to lure

any hoodie or vixen scouring the hills. Eyes
intact, they have not lain long. The air
acrid, we give them a wide berth. Meanwhile
on the sparse slopes, querulous sheep graze.

Aria

Three feet down, in the clarity of Loch Eddy,
a rainbow trout sluggishly avoids the fly
on offer. Our rowing-boat drifts on, with scarcely

a ripple. Suddenly the surface quivers:
the fish leaps into the air, then splashes
back on its belly. As though you, lying there

in drugged sleep, were totally to ignore
my kisses, a moment later to reappear
singing an aria from *Così fan Tutti*.

The Boathouse

The boathouse is the worse for wear: cracked
pantiles let in rain; a shutter is unhinged, the pocked
weather-vane broken by some local sharp-shooter.
The landing-stage too has seen better days,
its boards rotting. Yet we visit whenever we can
this fading Estate, skirting the big house
and the love temple, with its beeches and planned
rhododendrons. One man has taken the place of eight
gamekeepers. Nor do minor Royalty come as they did,
to bag the occasional deer or hold their swinging parties.

Envisage the locals, deferential; the young
gentry, on holiday from boarding school
in the south, disporting themselves nightly.
See the ice-buckets bead, the champagne flow.
The wendy-house on the island, overgrown now,
must have held many a Chekhovian scene,
or Bacchanalian, girls with flimsy dresses,
hair gossamer in the breeze; sheep's carcasses,
breeding maggots on which the brown trout fed,
straddled on wires, across the water's surface.

Strange that our presence should overlay theirs
as we manoeuvre our clinker-built boat in pursuit
of stocked rainbows where, in early summer,
the mountain-ash extend their candelabra.
What will the future bring? Can one owner
with propriety retain such inherited *grandeur*?
Yet how transfer so inaccessible a property,
as some would decree, to the down-trodden?
No ready solution. Our own, who knows,
may come to be counted among 'those balmy days'.

Two Harrier jets wheel overhead; a reminder
of other priorities. Their roar lingers
long after they disappear. Time to row in.
The boathouse shimmers, in the aftermath of rain.
A mink, predator of a different order,
swims to the bank, a fish in its jaws.
In the subsequent near-silence,
intensified by our bow-ripple, I realise
we have not seen or heard the peregrine,
this season: like ourselves, an endangered species.

Bird Songs

Starling

Leave me be, to chirp those
notes natural to me. Why should I
aspire to the nightingale's RP,
the career cadences
of thrush and blackie?

I'm merely the back-court piper
of gable walls, fag-end
of a raucous tradition;
chatterer on roof-trees –
see it how you please.

Nor am I wholly aloof: the others
may not be my cup of tea,
but I'll sit on a telegraph-wire
all day, listening happily
as their songs pass me by.

Bittern

Think of the years I threw away, down there,
intent on selling my wares, when all they cared for

was the phoney falsetto of canaries in cages,
or at a pinch, the Home Counties' dawn chorus –

twitterers in hedgerows. Such expenditure
of energy: I'd have changed register

even, to fit in. But those days are gone.
Life began again, when I joined the brass section.

Resident

Finding a convenient five-barred gate
I hitch a trouser-leg up and adopt
a proprietorial pose. Trouble is,
I can't keep my face straight.

For one thing I haven't the right garb,
and however levelly I gaze out
am not even an absentee landlord,
more a temporary tenant, this visit.

That apart I still carry the flab
I'm here to get rid of. I'll acclimatise
as soon as my boots are broken in
and the war with the horse-flies is won.

Conspicuous meantime, in a landscape
complete without me, I'll make a start
by cutting the grass, in the hope
of damping that wren's derisive flute.

Bird of Passage

(for Tom Leonard)

ALEXANDER WILSON: *b*. Paisley, Scotland 1766;
d. Southwark, Philadelphia 1813

The starlings that roosted in Paisley Abbey's
squat hulk, accumulating layers of lime,
have long since gone, without recognising
the *rara avis* to whom late last century
a statue was raised: Alexander Wilson,
who flew through life like a highly coloured bird.

For chastising such silky muck-worms
as his Hollander who resisted Reform,
and scoun'rel Shark, trig in his powdered
wig, measures fixed to cheat his weavers,
Wilson was hounded by a less than enamoured
constabulary. Plucking his tail feathers,

they locked him in the tolbooth; his verses,
a friend to Liberty, suppressed and burnt.
After Thomas Muir's transportation,
the judiciary preparing its grapeshot,
he felt it wise to jump bail, sailing by way
of Portpatrick and Belfast for Philadelphia.

Jack-of-all-trades but unable to endure
life's collisions, he scraped a living; till
he fell for the warbler's song, the allure
of orchard orioles, their nests suspended
from twigs on fibre hooked and wound
with an ingenuity he, a weaver, had to admire.

Warming to the task of a lifetime
he persuaded a publisher to take on
his magnum opus, *Birds of America*;
seeking subscribers by horse and canoe,
from the St Lawrence to the Mississippi;
meeting Jefferson and Thomas Paine.

A woodpecker, locked in his Wilmington
hotel-room, made a start on a mahogany table;
while a kite, sinking a talon to the bone
and released by severing a sinew of its heel,
confirmed *its* existence. A phantom
flycatcher, his sole aberration, purloined

by Audubon. Father of American Ornithology,
did he ponder the perplexed cartography
of Renfrewshire; engravings untinted,
new species unnoted, had he not departed?
Later, as he lay dying from dysentry
brought on by swimming in pursuit

of a wounded plover, did his thoughts migrate
to the Abbey grounds where he stands
opposite Robert Tannahill, friend
and fellow-poet, who unable to find a publisher
stepped into the Candren Burn, top-coat
folded on the bank, silver fob-watch beside it?

Family Tree

'And wha shall be able ta staun
Prepared for the great Bridal feast,
Only they wha obey the command
And escape the mark o the Beast.

It will come like the crack o a gun
And the door for ever clink tae.
Few, few shall hear the well done
And the many be left ta their wae.'

In faded photographs, vanished generations
display shovel beards and gold watch-chains.
Here and there a sheepish smile; but in the main
they confront the future with old-fashioned
steadfastness of gaze. Flanked by cousins, austere
in their Sunday best, stands my great-uncle
Todd Cochrane, supplier of horses to the Cavalry
during World War I – whom as a boy I imagined
careering round Ayrshire astride one of his stallions.
Churchill to him a warmonger, Stalin the Red
Dragon of the Apocalypse, he'd recite chapter
and verse, the big Bible on his knee;
once sacking a land-girl for whistling
on the sabbath. Charged by the Holy Ghost,
he and his sisters burst in on my father,
studying for the ministry, to announce the Second
Coming of Christ. The War over, a voice
from Heaven assured them the World would end
at noon next day: would he climb Craigie Hill
with them, to pray. They succeeded, unaided,
in keeping the last trump at bay; thereafter
going into retreat, Martha staying 'with friends'
for a spell; the matter unlikely to have been
spoken of again had not Todd, on his death-bed,
complained of '…live coals, in the brain'.

Craggy Country

Tales of Craigie Hill occupy my memory:
how at Mungo Farquhar's corner a pony
and trap, come recklessly adrift, sent driver
and passenger plummeting; the crazed beast,
flecked with foam, finally caught and quietened
outside the creamery, at Riccarton road-end.

I would think of this, as among empty churns
or clinging to the tail-gate, I ascended
through morning mist to the farm: those
earlier generations like speeded-up figures
in Chaplin films; the frame frozen on Sundays,
men's boots gleaming, women in black lace.

Later, on my second-hand Raleigh racer
with drop handle-bars, I'd zigzag uphill,
squirming on the narrow saddle; on the return
journey imagining myself the first Scotsman
ever to win the Tour de France. Once,
eager to catch the cricket at Kirkstyle,

I cut things too fine and leaving my machine
described an arc in mid-air, in slow motion,
before landing; then headed painfully home
with the crumpled wheels and buckled frame
all grass and mud – object of derision
as townie come a cropper, or country buffoon.

Illusionists

The Great Levant could make an elephant appear
where there had been thin air, a moment before.

Robert Houdin would saw his blonde assistant in half,
then restore her 'before your very eyes'. Easy to laugh

now, at the sleazy razzmatazz – because we know
it was all done with mirrors; or recall the row

we sat in, in Kilmarnock's Palace Theatre,
while a 'volunteer' vouched for a fiver

that the blunt-edged sword-ladder
Kalanag climbed barefoot was sharp as a razor.

So my wonder-box, its fluttering silk squares,
the snowman ghost-tube stocked with spring flowers,

even the gleaming dove-pans, ultimately
lost their allure and were given away.

But I remember Chung Ling Soo used to catch a bullet
fired across the stage, in his teeth: until one night

he was accidentally shot in the head. How ironic
with his final trick, to prove Death no fake.

Janàček Quartet

As we listen the virtuosity
of the music quickens, its frenzy

catching love's expectancy;
then gives way to the reverie

conveying the features
of the girl he'd fallen for.

For me it is yours,
not hers, it captures:

so that I too would rather
it were on the *viola d'amore*.

The Eye-Shade

Finding this eye-shade on the kitchen table
and putting it on, I am able

for the first time to counteract the glare
from the desk-light in my study. Your father

wore it latterly, to protect failing eyesight.
Now in minute part, I can inhabit

his world, gauge its curve, grow sensitive
to its more manageable perspective.

His spectrum, we knew, had been restricted;
his Emerald Isle made more so, as predicted –

each image on his television screen,
not only grass and baize, reduced to green.

The eye-shade would have been appropriate
if, earlier, he could have worn it

when burning the midnight oil, as editor
of the Abbey's monthly newsletter.

Truly, what intervening object can impede
the vision of the good? Nor can his shade

do us harm, if it focuses the mind on others,
or induces an old age in which like him we conquer,

with verve and humour, bereavement and despair:
a lovely man, most distant yet most dear.

Butterfly Farm

'Within this animal group with its reputation
for irritation, disease and destruction,

exist some of the most captivating creatures
on Earth': not Man – but the 170,000 species

of moths and butterflies comprising the order
Lepidoptera. The word conjures up ladies

in long skirts, eccentric professors,
rows of bodies transfixed under glass cases.

The butterfly farm repudiates this picture.
The air vibrant with patterns and colour,

in a tropical environment exotic larvae
pursue their daily routine, silky pupae emerge to beauty:

Common Grass Yellow, Great Orange Tip, Blue Swallowtail,
all here, along with Monarch, crepuscular Owl.

An order exists, secure under nets,
which we might envy, given the threats

our world presents. But how safe would we be,
even if protected from the equivalent of birds that fly

and free to flutter like these, with only Chinese quails
harmlessly grubbing below, puffballs on wheels?

Two Poems
(for Norman MacCaig, on his 80th birthday)

Profile

Like a ship's prow
cleaving dark waters, imagine him,
gliding into Lochinver
leaving a phosphorescent trail.

Or more at home still, on Suilven,
aslant to the wind;
no mists unsettling
that lucid mind.

The skull could be weathered stone,
but too thinking, feeling.
Paradox: a mountain peak
itself a source of light.

Odd looking back, the attempts
to scotch him – who undeviating
has enriched Scottishness
through its encompassing him.

Nor one for pomposity
he could turn plaudits topsy-turvy;
with deserved laurels crowned,
might munch the leaves, one by one.

Suilven

After a long day
on obdurate lochans
I ended up unable to see
for driving rain,
and night falling.

Suddenly there loomed
over me an outcrop
stern and uncanny,
yet vaguely familiar:
not Wordsworth's craggy

steep, or the Brocken
(conditions were wrong)
but MacCaig's profile
a mile high,
where Suilven had been.

This of course his territory.
From the peat-track,
I looked back:
on the horizon
was Suilven again;

but glancing
on the lochans between,
a luminescence
I could only call
the ghost of a smile.

Manzù Exhibition, Last Afternoon

His style is necessarily figurative because the figure, as an entity in its own
right, is the pivot around which Manzù's pictorial world moves.
GIULIO CARLO ARGAN

Do I see you through his eyes or my own,
fragile girl poised on the rim of a chair
too high for you? For what house-party or play
were you dressing up? Such haughtiness of expression,
mouth turned down at the corners, eyes
with a Japanese slant, you seem simultaneously

come-hitherish and shy, as if saying, 'Capture
I defy you, the evanescence of this moment':
which is precisely what the sculptor has done.
Closing time approaches. Uniformed attendants
unhinge wooden shutters. Footsteps click
on the polished floor as hushed visitors,

ourselves among them, scurry for a last glimpse
of a favourite piece – with in the centre room
that slouched Cardinal, dominant as on a throne.
Reverberant doors slam. Rather than imagine
the sculptures imprisoned in darkness,
alone, I sense the pervading presence

of an elderly man in an accustomed jacket
and soft hat; hands, unable to dissimulate,
kneading clay like dough: so intense
the humanity with which he imbues
his figures, they resonate in the memory –
incomparable bronzes, lubricated by light.

Picture Framer

He takes a sliver of powdered gold,
specially prepared; extends it
on a knife-blade, steady handed
and scarcely daring to breathe,
over the frame he is working on;

then with a simultaneous
exhalation and practised
flip of the wrist, sends
it floating – to land face up
on precisely the right spot:

the gesture repeated,
with what seems
sublime indifference,
till the task is complete;
the frame lustrous, immaculate.

So is love, even after
a lifetime's experience,
at the mercy of flights
as hazardous as those
of gold leaf, through draughts of air.

Intimate Letter
(for Mary Munro)

At the approach of Christmas we cling to fortune's
wheel, aware of what has befallen those cabins
of twisted steel; the corpses cruelly strewn,
identified by relatives newly flown in.

Pity tempered by relief, we try to comprehend
the pain; pray we never succumb to such atrocity.
By comparison you seemed, as though determined
to trouble no one, to die almost effortlessly,

when the end came. Yet the lowering of your coffin,
coinciding with so many bereaved ones
hearing God's Word or the howl of a barren wind,
revealed a transforming courage of its own –

so that tenderly supplanting the savagery
of this fearful time, I glimpse in my mind's eye
a grandmother and granddaughter, hand in hand
beside an otter sculpture, overlooking Solway.

Breach of Privacy

In today's paper is a close-up of a boy
orphaned by the disaster at Lockerbie,
supported at his sister's graveside
by family friends, and vacant-eyed.

How at such a time dare a lens intrude?
Could not we be trusted
privately to proffer a prayer
without prying on his despair?

Does his now appearing here
render me, in turn, a *voyeur*?
I would but entreat life
ease rather than trespass on his grief.

Skye Poems
(for Bar and John Purser)

On arrival

Here for a break, to shake the mind free
from its dullness, I gaze out on a sea
alternately dazzling with troughs of light
and lost in mist. As I sit and write
you work away, literally overhead,

scraping the cottage's corrugations
with an old hoe, prior to applying tar.
Your implement grates and grates, so close
I feel I am a turtle or some such creature
having its shell cleaned, barnacles forcibly

removed, with the detritus of the past.
Below, the Bay glistens fitfully.
Bright thoughts force an entry. Soon
the new man that I am must venture
outside, skull scoured, legs however unsteady.

Dawn, Drinan

I lie dozing, in the early hours,
aware of some element missing.
Then it comes: a burst of hail
blattering on the corrugated iron
of the roof, like a blizzard
of rock-fragments, before expending
itself on the shore at Kilmarie.

Dizzied, I recall the scramble
from Coir an Lochain to the ridge;
our straddling Sgurr Dubh na Da Bheinn,
a sheer drop beyond. The shower passes
as unexpectedly as it came.
Opening my eyes I see the room re-form,
the curtain opposite slowly redden.

Reminder

What remains of today's skyline
is enhanced or marred, according
to viewpoint, by this home-made chair:
roofed over in Spartan fashion,
its circular peep-holes enable land
on one side, sea on the other,
to recur. Position it, climb in,
you have a sun-trap to boast of;
protection from inclement weather;
a bird-hide, for the eager visitor;
sentry-box even, its driftwood
thicker than any arrow-head. The one
concession to modernity – castors,
for mobility. Upended and fronted
it could prove an economic coffin,
were one to squat simply, not lie down.
Before leaving, I am to put it
in the peat-shed, for its proper safety.

Sabbath

Overnight the wind shifts
from south-west to north-east:
we are into a new season.
The Tourist Board seals
sunning themselves in Loch Slapin
have taken the money, and run.

Those mountains that looked as if
you could lean out and touch them
have come clean: they were
contours in the imagination.
The blueness of the other side
might have been invented.

And it's the sabbath. Well, serve
it right – all week the Blackface
have been looking down their noses
like Wee Frees, at a spritely pigeon
with a birch-twig in its beak
masquerading as a dove of peace.

The islanders to the newly-weds

This gift is for you, its graded shades
of grey drawn one from each breed
of sheep on our Island – the wool undyed.

It will require to be teased and spun,
thereafter woven to whichever design
meets your fancy. Before then,

there are the proper means
of preparing the tweed. True romance
decrees the ritual of the dance:

place in a tub, cover with water;
then tread with vigour, the pair
of you, for not less than eight hours.

During the process, such activity
permitted as conforms with propriety.
We wish you happiness. And energy.

Bog myrtle

Evenly spread on bunk beds
in the room above, bog-myrtle lay
drying – till it was taken south

for beer-making. What lingers
is its scent – so that I imagine
some young couple trysting here

(not Diarmid and Grainne, but a less
fated pair), a blessing on them:
legacy of its fragrance, in the air.

Meanwhile I'll leave this poem between
the sheets. Will it curl curiously,
or just fade away? We'll see.

October Week

Presence

On my first day back, I am drawn
towards Blaven. Despite driving rain
I park, put on wellington boots
and set out. As I leave the track
and rise above the tree-line, mists clear,
revealing an amber glare. Bog-myrtle,
crushed underfoot, releases its fragrance.
And I find my love for you, in absence,

grows more intense. If only, I feel,
by some miracle you could be here;
knowing even as I turn, spontaneously
eager, that it is a flight of fancy.
Except that, acknowledging where
I'd imagined you would be, over
Loch Slapin there rises one rainbow's
perfect arc, within the ghost of another.

The chair

This chair has seen two winters
since we were last here. In honesty,
give or take a few bare patches,
it resists the climate better than were I
left out in all Elgol weathers.

But wait. It has become lopsided.
A rocking-chair isn't what's wanted.
Each time I shift my weight
it seems to have a limp built in.
The last thing to sit a gin and tonic on.

This stone will keep you steady. In return
grant a few hours' rest, this visit
too. But should winter come early
I'll allow you a shoogle, to waken me,
lest they have to dig us both out.

Intruder

I've realised I am spending the week
with an older man. He comes downstairs
a hairsbreadth behind me; and when I go climbing
imposes his limits. For him I pack a spare
pullover, leave the immersion heater on.

Could it be the green woolly hat I found
in a lay-by? Perhaps it was planted
by trolls. This morning while shaving
I was confronted by a puckered frown
peering from under it, grey wisps protruding.

He keeps telling me I'm putting on weight;
but I'm damned if I'll let him impose his diet.
If he has to rise during the night, that's
his problem. And when the time comes,
he can do his own clearing up.

From the ridge

We huddle as though in the lee of a dyke,
where there is none: myself, and those
admonitory selves who urged, 'Stay in,
you'll be drenched before you even reach
the stream, which in any case won't be passable.
And if you try to cross at the waterfall,
you'll find the face sheer glass.'

They were right, of course. 'Furthermore,
you'll have to cling to the buttress,
lest a gust hurl you over.' Here
I last glimpsed a pair of eagles,
wheeling effortlessly over the scree,
past the impossible pinnacle. I hug
the ground, anticipate a squall.

Instead, a lull: with it, that break
in the clouds I feared would never come;
and miles away, the flat summit of Raasay,
where obsequious Boswell danced his jig.

Relic

The elk-skull in the adjoining room
remains untouched by my presence.
He is lord of this place,

sustaining not merely visions
of pursuit over rough terrain,
torrents taken in their stride,

but the tremor of millenia
in the span of those antlers
before the hounds of Cuchulain;

flanks that covered bogland
when Scotland and Ireland were one.
When I go, I leave all to him.

W.S. Graham

I imagine you, somewhere
   in the woods near Madron,
waiting for the barn-owls to flutter
   and whoo, then swoop down

to take you on yet
   another of these mysterious journeys
you will tell us about
   later, your phrases

so perfectly turned and weightless
   they'd defy gravity
but for the ice
   that pins them in place. Sydney,

I wish you well, this
   night and any other
as in your thermal you rise
   through thin air – or

far out from the coast
   in a different manner
find yourself driving the last
   tram, from There to Here.

Renewal Notice

Our renewal notice offers cover
against falling trees, hitherto
act of God. A few nights ago
next door's sycamore narrowly
missed. What of the roar
at seances, similar
to crumbling upper storeys?

We hear on the News
of doors burst open,
three elders gunned down,
women and children maimed;
calls for retaliation
we cannot condone –
yet do not utterly condemn.

Next day, not even Corelli
unravelling on Radio 3
can erase from the mind
those worshippers crouched behind
flimsy pews in a pentecostal hall.
The blue sky appallingly banal,
shears snipping, you trim the ivy on the wall.

Three Poems

Accessories

In my wallet I carry a tiny
St Christopher medal; round
my neck on a chain, a half-moon,
part talisman, part wedding-band:

these and my wife's jewellery
reminders of places and events
accumulated over the years;
each preserving minutely

an aspect of identity. Tonight
we see them in a changed light
which penetrates to the heart,
having attended the funeral

of a godson who prior to a car
accident had collected a ring,
gifted for his twenty-first.
Such unendurable radiance.

Storm damage

In the grounds, branches broken
by recent gales are already sawn;
the residue of bonfires retaining
ample heat, to quicken into flame.

Beyond the pond, a dozen trees
encircle a horse's grave. Lie
on the grass and look up: high above
like plumes, tall cedars nod and weave

against a bustling sky. A week
later, I imagine I remain
prostrate, under their scrutiny;
having tapped an intensity

of grief, those days between:
as though only now great hooves,
drumming and drumming under the soil,
were settling, and becoming still.

Intricacies

Before he was any age, they'd set out
each morning for the rink at Richmond,
so that he could be on the ice by 6 a.m.

In subsequent years, he earned not only
the trophies adorning his room
but warmth of applause, a unique affection.

The ultimate barrier broken, things can never
be the same. From the heart's recesses
he goes flawlessly spinning, beneath boughs

bearing snow like blossom. Across
the limitless expanses of the imagination,
he pirouettes joyously – then is gone.

His skates' pure harmonies ring on and on.

Forth Bridge

The first definite record of the Black-browed Albatross in Scotland was in 1967, when one took up residence on the Bass Rock.
Thom: BIRDS IN SCOTLAND

Before the rampaging Trades thrust me off course
I thought I had seen it all: Antarctic palaces
like massifs of crystal; incandescent towers
rotating in space; geysers of quicksilver.
The switch of hemispheres let me witness

something more striking still: in a drizzly
landmass amidst dazzling haar, an edifice
so astounding I instantly based myself here:
no spindly wader, but big-shouldered, grid
of wing-quills; muscle straddling the Forth,

loftily dwarfing man. I spiral its thermals;
steel lattice caging the sun. Till a thrill
of terror: through its central span
a fiery tremor, as of girders brought down.
Bitter taste of my origin. Then dawned:

plated beasts, shuttling tinder trails;
no threat of the riveted mesh collapsing,
augmenting the past, bodies plummeting
to the estuary below. At that time
my smirched brows matched by a swart

deposit, drifting towards Fife's green
kingdom. In the face of an ominous
radiance, the yammerers jostling
for ledges come and go in their millions.
Superstition preserves the albatross.

So I celebrate this centenary; and craters
for eyes, croaking what praises I can,
dedicate my aerobatics, from pole-star
and southern cross, to the Leviathan
who designated me great lord of the Bass.

From Arthur's Seat

North-east the Firth, a bracelet
merging with mist; south-west
the Pentlands, sharply defined. Directly
opposite, the castle. A sudden gust
makes me lose my footing. Gulls slip past,
eyeing us disdainfully.
On lower ground, we find respite.

Strange to contemplate this spot,
gouged cleanly out,
as going back millions of years;
its saucer fire and ice, volcanic
rock shaped by glaciers,
where now cameras click
and lovers stroll in pairs.

Such thoughts cannot be further
from the minds of those golfers
on the fairway below, heads down
and eyes on the ball, oblivious
to the shadows
furtively closing in,
the imminence of rain.

Tempting, watching us
loll here, to deduce
the same; whereas
it is often when happiest,
we are most conscious
of darkness. See, it sweeps
towards us, the rim of an eclipse.

Unicorn Tapestries
(for Meta and Ian Gilmour)

Survival

Mediaeval in origin, their preservation a marvel,
gracing La Rochefoucauld's château at Verteuil
until the Revolution, these exquisite tapestries
were purloined – then found fortuitously in a barn,
protecting potatoes for a starving peasantry.

Millefleurs

The tapestries burgeon
with spring flowers: primroses,
known as St Peter's keys;
field daisies in profusion

called 'eye of Christ', cure
for excessive desire
leading to infidelity;
marigold and clary,

the latter with honey
a remedy for poison;
yellow-flag, reputedly
easing the pains of pregnancy.

Paddling towards these,
intent on his prey:
a scenting hound, collar
adorned with *fleurs-de-lys*.

And in this sombre corner, see
coiled the periwinkle, 'joy
of the ground': effective
against snake-bite

and, antidote to spite,
able to dispel discord between
man and wife. Carry it
constantly on your person

that it may give immunity
from the devil's influence
and – greatest gift of all –
ensure freedom from terror.

Signaller

They advance, thinking they are unseen;
whereas motionless behind my screen
of walnut, linden, aspen and blue plum,
I observe the gloating expressions
of dog-handlers and brocaded Seigneurs,

young noblemen in sumptuous outfits
high-stepping it, a jaunty
page-boy pointing gleefully
that the quarry has been sighted.
Not all are participants: witness

the compassion of the old huntsman,
fur hat tied under his chin.
Yet so immediate the brutality,
alongside richness and beauty,
that rather than peer across a chasm

of centuries, you fear to see mirrored
your innermost features: while marvelling
at such floral profusion,
you huddle in your soft-lit ring,
eyes restless, pale faces signalling.

Aftermath

Having visited the Cloisters
with their millefleurs tapestries,
we walk through Central Park. Shadows
lengthening, black acrobats

on skateboards, making bird noises,
accelerate from an underpass.
I grasp your hand, try not to run.
Behind sparse shrubbery, huntsmen

hack with pikes; hounds, leashes
slipped, pant with exertion. Could we,
finding a unicorn in the thorny dark,
do more than the mediaeval herbalist

who in his time of turbulence
prescribed, for mad dogs and others,
distilled primrose water
as a calming influence?

II.

The Luncheon of the Boating Party

1 *Alphonse*

'Have you nothing better to do?', calls
my father, not discreetly, as would befit
my station (son of the proprietor, after all)
but in a blacksmith's bellow, spittle flecking
his chin: 'These boats need repairing.' Instead

I lean on the balustrade, observer and observed,
posing for a painting. (When will he understand
it is not seemly to move, once positioned?)
By an artisan too, no mistake about it:
a true painter who finds the term 'artist' effete.

How long it could take, God knows. Some *cocotte*
wrote asking to be in it. When she found Angèle
already here, the fur flew. 'Snotty bitch!'
'Just because you sat for Degas!' From our upper
terrace come their voices, across four decades.

And all illusion: the fourteen of us
were never together at the one time, far less
spaciously composed. That aside, why make me
so severe; and Caillebotte, seated opposite,
conspicuously fresh-faced? Not that I'm other

than proud to be there: look how many (a Baron
included) were required, to counterbalance me.
Most astounding, the light: no criss-cross of shade
under the striped awning, but a constant suffusion.
The way he depicts it forces me to re-remember.

'That must be the boatman,' I suddenly overhear,
'waiting till luncheon's over, to ply his trade.'
'Or Charon, envisaging the placing of coins,
in due time.' Not dreaming I'd catch the reference;
or realising how, uppermost in my mind

and complementing these succulent flesh-tones,
was Renoir's skin, even then tightening on his bones
like canvas stretched over the frame of a painting;
as in one of those pleasure-boats, long-since gone,
he would sit, to be rowed across the dappled Seine.

2 *The Baron*

Why should he complain? What about me?
The back of my head's about all you see,
and precious little else. Whereas if he'd chosen,
Renoir my dear old pal, to survey the scene
from the other end of the terrace, I'd have been

smack in the centre. With his back to the Seine,
I mean. Then he could have called his painting
'Baron Barbier, ex-cavalry officer and bohemian,
lunching with friends at the Restaurant Fournaise':
if I had been presented full phiz, that is,

not in this retiring fashion. Between you and me,
I was in fact facing him, when he began. Only
to let myself be distracted by that 'unknown
model' (as the catalogue calls her) leaning over
the balustrade, ogling in my direction.

Actually her name was Maxine. I could fill you in
more fully, if you want, but don't see why
I should do her any favours, when she did me none.
There she is, a nonentity preserved for posterity,
whereas I am virtually relegated to 'Anon'.

And in one of the finest paintings ever painted,
it would seem. Not that anyone dreamt that,
at the time. Indeed when the moment came
to cough up, Monsieur Balensi (it seems) reneged
on the deal. I thought she was egging me on

(Maxine, that is) but it turned out all she was after
was what she could glean about my friend Maupassant.
As for that haughty buffoon, the proprietor's son
(yes, back to him again) let me tell you something.
He was damn near not even in the picture. Renoir

painted him out, then in again, after asking him
to take off his jacket and wear a white singlet.
And do you know why? In order to highlight
the flowers on a straw hat. As though we existed
purely for his still life. What do you make of that?

3 *Unknown Man*

'Out there' they said, 'on the terrace –
you're wanted.' When I heard the din
I assumed it was those oarsmen again,
kicking up a shindig. Not a bit of it –
there were some of the regulars,

and a man with a pointy beard,
painting them. 'That's perfect' he said,
'don't worry about your arms, so long
as you face in this direction.' I was only
a bit player, I realise. All the same

it was fun, to be one of them.
I well remember the conversation –
even the chaps whispering smutty jokes
to the girl with black gloves.
At one stage she covered her ears,

from embarrassment. I could tell
they were both trying to get off
with her. But Renoir made it look
as though she was straightening her hat.
What a pure spirit, to go through life

confronted by all those nudes –
complete waste, ask me. Mind you
he did, even then, have a crush
on the girl with flowers in her hat,
and married her later, I gather.

Anyway, we were simply a job-lot
transformed by his painting. One laugh:
as fast as the wine went down,
his brush replenished it: Art can't
get more practical, than that.

As for the fellow in the top-hat,
I couldn't make out a word
he said. Might have been
from another planet. Mind you,
it was a magical afternoon...

4 *Madame Renoir*

Curiously enough, seeing that picture again
awakens in me not visuals so much as fragrances:
the bouquet of red wine, those grapes and peaches
in the dish under my nose; Alphonse's breath
from over my shoulder, as he munches garlic;

and the mustiness of that stupid little dog
Renoir made me hold: I'm sure it gave me fleas.
Maggiolo poured wine down its throat
for a joke – not expecting it to get its own back,
which it did, biting his finger to the bone.

It must have been all in his head, from the start.
Not that you'd have known. Empty glasses and litter
everywhere; the clash of cutlery, bottles quivering...
Oh yes – the women's perfume, that comes back;
Angèle's lily-of-the-valley, something of the sort;

Ellen's sultry and spicy, like bruised fruit.
I wore rose-water, which I knew Renoir fancied.
'It makes a unity of the senses' he said,
'with the flowers adorning your hat;
symbol of maidenhood.' I was naive enough

to believe him, I think. How ironic,
to be preserved on canvas, in full bloom,
while the body fails – most of all that
of our creator; hands deformed, the brush
strapped to his wrist, with bandages,

that he might paint. A whole world has gone,
never to return. Including those luxurious
days at Chatou. He always worked from the heart;
gave more than he took. Despite what they say
about him not paying his models: why should he,

when he was making them eternal?
As for me, that time is best recaptured
when I sit beside him in his wicker chair
and sense in his eyes – despite the pain –
a loving tenacity: light glancing on water.

5 *Renoir*

Coarse blotches, suggestive of putrescent flesh,
was how they described my "impressions"
in those early days. No wonder every so often,
Monet and I to escape would stuff ourselves
with larded turkey, washed down with Chambertin.

They protested, 'How can we go by other
than what is seen?' Oblivious
(so much for their breadth of vision)
that the eye ultimately sees
not through itself, but by some other thing.

54

(What shame anyway, in feasting heart *and* eye?)
Further irony, in my never contriving to be
the revolutionary they would have preferred me.
My dream of harmony, not anarchy, all these years
I tried simply to mirror nature; to give joy.

Then there were those, who in my intoxication
with female flesh saw an unbridled passion
mirroring some lust of their own – whereas
detecting in breasts and buttocks a purity as well
as beauty, I caressed with brush-strokes alone.

Their trouble, that they allow only one shade
of black, to indulge their curdled spirits.
Ignoring the shadowy presence of blues and greens
which delight the senses, they deride red's redness;
any notion of colour sounding like a bell.

In years to come, carping critics forgotten,
my portraits will sing of Angèle and Ellen,
Gabrielle and Suzanne. If nothing else,
I will have preserved them on canvas: my strength,
and weakness. Meantime, my beloved already gone,

I find it difficult to recollect those days.
Lying twisted under this wire contraption,
I watch the bones work their way through my skin.
Soon, I shall be beyond pain. All labour done,
there will be no paints to mix, no brushes to clean.

At Les Collettes
(for Serge Baudot)

Scarcely any distance from the peopled *plages*
extending their pebbled curve to Menton
and beyond, under the broiling Mediterranean sun,
leave the boulevard and climb by the Passage Renoir
to *Les Collettes*, built for my final years.

In the hour before the house opens for the afternoon,
stroll round the gardens, under those knotted olives,
themselves a vast age before we came to occupy the place.
Shade your eyes, as I had to, and look across
the chasm of light between here and the château

at Cagnes. Imagine me, being wheeled down
these paths in my wooden chair, or sitting hunched
over that day's canvas, in my open-air studio.
Then enter the house, and experience its coolness.
Go up (as I could not, latterly, unaided)

to the *atelier* on the first floor, and look down
as I constantly did, on the powdery green
of the olive-trees. Consider them, if you care,
with their gnarled contortions, a metaphor
for my deformed hands' durability, through pain.

*

Fortunately I had too much to keep me busy
to worry about Cézanne and Matisse and the others
changing the face of Art. As I gather
turned out the case. I always kept to a sole design;
whereas they saw from several vantage points, at once.

Not only that, but they'd detect prisms
and angles, where I'd see only smoothness.
I sometimes wondered what chaos it could lead to –
especially when that dark-eyed young fellow Picasso
(born the year I did my *Déjeuner des Canotiers*)

came bounding like a goat, on the scene,
promising to go further even than their extremes;
painting what he thinks, not what he sees.
One clear reason why, rather than contemplate
the future, I was happy to remain in the present.

For all that I admit (in trust) to a desperation
that once what is new has been superceded
by the "new" new, my early work, derided
at the time, may be seen in truer perspective;
it be conceded I opened shutters, let light in.

*

Sleep comes over me. I have been too much in the sun.
And begin to be overtaken by some kind of delirium.
Purveyor of order, resident in this rectilinear mansion,
so meticulously terraced, I see myself at times
as comprising a geometry of my own: a sundial

round whom revolve fragrances, subtleties
of brightness and shade, which I transmute
to canvas, in a process most easily
attributed to sheer *joie de vivre* –
if only to put the culture hounds off the scent.

They could not comprehend, for instance, how Aline
dictated her own style. Not least, through my delight
in her rotundity: midway between fantasy
and reality. More splendidly too, than with any
other model, her skin responded to the light.

Even that, now a secondary consideration.
I miss her so much. Above all, the softness
of her fingers, as she wound the bandages on.
This, among my memories, the one thing
that dulls the pain. I wish she were with me again.

Renoir in Orkney

(for George Mackay Brown)

Monet might have made himself at home
among these flat, green islands
like giant water lilies. Cézanne even,
with cliff-faces all cones and cylinders.

Not that my vision is impaired.
More a narrowing of the spectrum
to a harmony of glistening silk,
as though too much light were being let in –

but without the embracing warmth
to which I am accustomed: seascape
and skyscape, a constant radiance.
It would need the skin of the place

to burst a blood vessel, or myself
to stab at it with my palette knife:
then there'd be something I could express.
Only this morning, the world disappeared;

the boat I was in surrounded
by quicksilver; the bordering land
erased in mist. Like a composer
frantic for some variation

beyond a single high-pitched note
sustained in his brain,
I crave a cacophony of colour,
before my mind disintegrates.

At least with the fishermen
I am at home. Their tanned features
merit the mixing of pigments:
my yellows and reds are in business again.

As for the womenfolk, baiting the line
has made their fingers like my own,
and worse: knife-gashes, to the bone.
Nudes are out. For one thing, their Kirk

concedes no such tradition.
For another, contemplate the climate.
But something in me burns. I must
start again. I have found a girl

with skin like mother-of-pearl;
am working on still lives of lobsters;
and will distribute at the solstice
canvases of wild flowers, like mottled flame.

Transformation

It wasn't the Mediterranean,
the yachts on the horizon,

the *bouillabaisse* and *cassis* even
which completed our *transformation:*

the ultimate confirmation
that *tout va bien* came,

after *un bon repas,*
in the *rue Pourquoi-pas.*

Fort Napoleon

We sit entranced in the night air,
watching a troupe of eight
actresses alternate as Alice.

The dew so heavy they slither
on the stage, till one goes barefoot,
and the others follow suit. Finally

they vanish, leaving only the moon's
refractions, and a filigree
of drenched prints, where they had been.

Military Museum

Toulon basks below. A red box-kite strains
at its wire, a cliché of aspiration,
giving song to the wind. On the summit
of le Faron is a military museum, complete
with simulations of the Allied landings
in World War Two. Coloured bulbs flicker
on a cartographic screen, at each site taken.
On stereo speakers, crackly bombers roar.

So many souls lost, but how few their number
when set against a nuclear future.
Covering the walls of the tower, these
framed photographs, medals for valour,
letters of condolence, regimental colours,
are like the outmoded weapons ambiguous
reminders of values valiantly fought for.
Consider their selflessness, the readiness

to sacrifice themselves, that their children
might inherit a land free from war. For us:
how preserve the pride nationhood engenders
yet encompass the call for wider loyalties,
thereby surmounting the barriers between men's
minds? Such power, to decree not only what *is*,
but what will one day be. Nor assurance
as to the outcome of human struggle: witness

the sacking of Troy by deceitful Greece,
lots drawn for princess and queen; the murder
of Agamemnon, restoration of the old order;
the founding of Rome. No place for arrogance,
in history's progress: down the centuries
the classic flaw for consecutive conquerors,
to think their rule pre-ordained, or God-given,
who renege on their duty to their fellow men.

Monflanquin

We follow the track to Monflanquin,
on either side the sheen of rippling grain,
past the graveyard with its flaked stone

and flowers preserved under bell-jars.
As we stand there, a coach drawn by white horses
glides past. Is that the music of the spheres

and is it too part of a fantasy,
like the quivering pantiles, the sky
too blue to be real? Try though we may,

it is difficult in such an atmosphere
to realise we are no longer
the definitive selves we once were.

Such timelessness cannot last.
Before they go to waste
or become things of the past

on our return to more mundane
surroundings, the diurnal routine,
within us let us jealously retain

those moments by that honey-coloured château
where we stood arm in arm, as from an upper window
came soaring the overture to *The Marriage of Figaro*.

Lot-et-Garonne

This the domain of fable, of ant and grasshopper,
invisible cicada and cackling jay. Facing
due east, the sunflowers shrivel. Over meadows
of maize, loop liquescent catherine-wheels.
Meanwhile in the arena between my feet
two crimson beetles, linked tail to tail,
tug one another across cracked soil.

Surfeit of fruit; a season's abundance:
nectarine and peach in profusion; bruised
melon, going cheap. So we stroll, and buy.
Bergerac for today's trout, *vin-de-table*
for tomorrow's *ragout*. Cheeses too, *du pays*.
But keep being drawn to those fruit vendors,
bare arms steeped in wasp-teeming wares.

An hour's cycle-run through shaded groves,
the Château de Biron emerges dominant
on the skyline, visible for miles around.
Severe but for its chapels. Its most
renowned Seigneur beheaded by Henri IV:
now centuries later, bleached bone
in blood-drenched soil. The sky porcelain.

Below, Lacapelle-Biron bakes. Our bicycles
against a wall, we bring out water-bottles
to slake our thirst. Under cypresses, solitary
Protestants lie. The air resonates, like a bell.
A woman waters begonias; while across the square,
a sandstone dog grins – his haunches
so yellow, he could be carved from butter.

A dragonfly settles on my shoulder, a flicker
of azure. Even under lime and acacia,
the glare becomes scarcely tolerable. Last
night's thunder did not long clear the air.
So much, so soon to be distanced from.
Already in the orchard has begun
the steady thud-thud of ripe fruit falling.